HorrorScapes

Voodoo in New Orleans

by Stephen Person

Consultant: Troy Taylor
President of the American Ghost Society
Author of *Haunted New Orleans: Ghosts &
Hauntings of the Crescent City*

BEARPORT
PUBLISHING

New York, New York

Credits

Cover and title page illustration by Dawn Beard Creative and Kim Jones; 4–5, Kim Jones; 6–7, Kim Jones; 8L, © ekash/iStockphoto; 8R, © Jerry Tavin/Everett Collection; 9, © Niday Picture Library/Alamy; 10, Kim Jones; 11, © Angelo Cavalli/SuperStock; 12, © Carolina Gonzalez; 13, © David Zentz/Alamy; 14, © Collection of the Louisiana State Museum, Marie Laveau by Franck Schneider ca 1915 after a painting attributed to George Catlin; 15L, © Jeff Greenberg/Omni-Photo; 15R, © Webstream/Alamy; 16, Kim Jones; 17L, © Steve Vidler/SuperStock; 17R, © Ariy/Shutterstock; 18, © Bob Sacha/Corbis; 19, © Daniel Heuclin/NHPA/Photoshot; 20, © Steve Parry/Imagestate Media Partners Limited/Impact Photos/Alamy; 21, © Jim West; 22, © Jeremy Woodhouse/SuperStock; 23, Kim Jones; 24–25, Kim Jones; 26, © Lee Foster/Lonely Planet Images; 27, © Stephano Buonamici; 28, Courtesy of The Library of Congress; 29T, © Anthony Collins/Fotolia; 29B, Courtesy of NOAA's National Weather Service (NWS) Collection; 30, © Caitlin Mirra/Shutterstock; 31, © Colin D. Young/Shutterstock.

Publisher: Kenn Goin
Editorial Director: Adam Siegel
Creative Director: Spencer Brinker
Design: Dawn Beard Creative and Kim Jones
Illustrations: Kim Jones
Photo Researcher: Omni-Photo Communications, Inc.

Library of Congress Cataloging-in-Publication Data

Person, Stephen.
  Voodoo in New Orleans / by Stephen Person.
      p. cm. — (HorrorScapes)
  Includes bibliographical references (p.   ) and index.
  ISBN-13: 978-1-936087-99-0 (library binding)
  ISBN-10: 1-936087-99-5 (library binding)
  1. Voodooism—Louisiana—New Orleans—History—Juvenile literature. 2. New Orleans (La.)—Religious life and customs—Juvenile literature. 3. Laveau, Marie, 1794–1881—Juvenile literature. I. Title.
  BL2490.P39 2011
  299.6'750976335—dc22

                            2010004976

For more information, write to Bearport Publishing Company, Inc., 101 Fifth Avenue, Suite 6R, New York, New York 10003. Printed in the United States of America in North Mankato, Minnesota.

072010
042110CGD

10 9 8 7 6 5 4 3 2 1

Contents

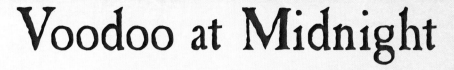

Voodoo at Midnight

It was a moonless night in New Orleans, Louisiana. The year was 1825. A young African American woman raced quietly through the dark, empty streets. She turned down an alley and finally saw what she was looking for—light coming from behind a half-opened door.

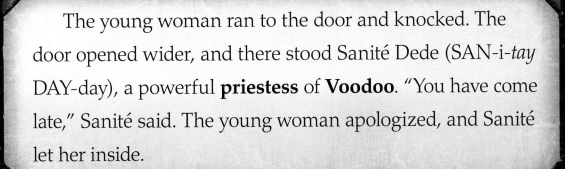

The young woman ran to the door and knocked. The door opened wider, and there stood Sanité Dede (SAN-i-*tay* DAY-day), a powerful **priestess** of **Voodoo**. "You have come late," Sanité said. The young woman apologized, and Sanité let her inside.

Sanité Dede was known as the "Voodoo Queen of New Orleans." This was a title given to the most powerful Voodoo priestess in the city.

5

The Right Place to Learn

Sanité led the young woman into a large room that was lit by the dancing flames of burning candles. About 60 people stood in the room—women and men, black and white, young and old. When Sanité gave a signal, the Voodoo ceremony began.

Music and dancing are important parts of Voodoo ceremonies. The goal of the ceremony is to contact the spirits of people who have died.

Several men started banging on drums. Another man lifted a huge red and black snake and called out, "Come, Voodoo, Voodoo!" This was a way of calling to the spirits of the dead. **Communication** with these spirits is an important part of Voodoo.

The young woman watched as people began to dance. She had come to Sanité Dede hoping to learn the secrets of the powerful Voodoo religion. She was in the right place.

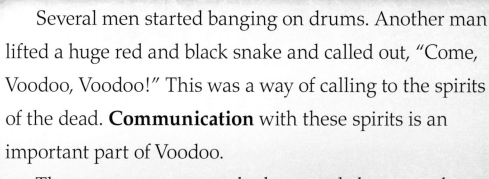

In Voodoo, a priestess is called "Queen" while a priest is called "Doctor." In the 1800s, the leaders of the Voodoo religion in New Orleans were nearly all women.

Life and Death in New Orleans

Even without midnight Voodoo ceremonies, New Orleans was an exciting city in the 1800s. The streets bustled with European and American **settlers**, **Native Americans**, free African Americans, and slaves. **Peddlers** pulled carts through the streets selling flowers, vegetables, and alligator meat. Days and nights were filled with operas, **balls**, parties, and parades.

New Orleans's rich mix of cultures, food, and music could be found nowhere else in the United States. Today, New Orleans is still considered one of the best cities in the country for great food, including jambalaya (left).

The French Opera House in New Orleans had seating for 2,000 people.

New Orleans was exciting, but deadly. Hurricanes and floods flattened homes. Human waste flowed in open **sewers**, and piles of trash rotted in the streets. All this filth allowed killer diseases such as **cholera** to spread quickly. With so many deaths, burials were common. To people's horror, however, dead bodies did not stay underground for long!

The Mississippi River flows through New Orleans. As a result, the city became a major shipping center.

New Orleans was founded by French settlers in 1718. It became part of the United States in 1803, when President Thomas Jefferson bought it from Napoleon, the ruler of France, as part of the **Louisiana Purchase**.

Louisiana Purchase

This map shows the area of the United States that Thomas Jefferson bought in the Louisiana Purchase.

9

Cities of the Dead

Why didn't the dead stay buried in New Orleans? The city was built on wet, low-lying land. In fact, about half the city is below **sea level**. As a result, when people were buried in the city's wet soil, underground water caused **caskets** and bodies to float back up through the ground. After heavy rains, bones and skulls popped out of the mud and glowed in the moonlight.

Bodies that were buried often oozed back up through the mud after a heavy rain.

Desperate for a solution to stop the floating bodies, people began building **tombs** above the ground. **Cemeteries** quickly became crowded with these small stone buildings. They became known as "cities of the dead." In New Orleans, many people believed that the dead lived on after death as spirits or ghosts. So it's easy to see why they thought the city was haunted.

This cemetery in New Orleans is made up of tombs that were built above the ground.

The cemeteries of New Orleans were, and still are, often visited by the living who are looking for answers from the dead.

From Africa to New Orleans

Spirits of the dead are a very important part of Voodoo. Voodoo is a religion that mixes African beliefs and traditions with the Catholic religion. It is based on the belief that spirits of the dead are all around people living on Earth. The goal of Voodoo is to contact these powerful spirits, and ask for their help.

Voodoo charms known as *gris-gris* (GREE-gree) are used to bring luck. One form of *gris-gris* is a small bag filled with everything from pepper and herbs to human fingernails and hair.

When worn around the neck, *gris-gris* bags like this one are said to protect the wearer.

The word *Voodoo* means "spirit" or "those who serve the spirits" in the language of the West African kingdom of Dahomey—now the country Benin (beh-NEEN). In the 1700s, slave traders captured thousands of people from this region and brought them to the United States. Some of the slaves were forced to work for families in New Orleans. Though they had lost their freedom, many held on to their religious beliefs and they began practicing Voodoo in New Orleans.

Enslaved Africans also brought Voodoo to Haiti, where it is still practiced today.

This map shows the country in Africa—Benin—where many of the slaves in New Orleans had been captured.

There Goes Marie Laveau!

In the 1820s, Sanité Dede was the Voodoo Queen of New Orleans. By 1830, there was a new queen—Marie Laveau (luh-VOH). Marie was tall and beautiful, with dark curly hair and glowing black eyes. When she walked down the street, her gold bracelets glittered. Her colorful skirts flowed in the breeze. "There goes Marie Laveau!" people would say. "That's the most powerful woman there is!"

Marie Laveau was born in New Orleans in 1801. Many people believe she learned Voodoo directly from Sanité Dede.

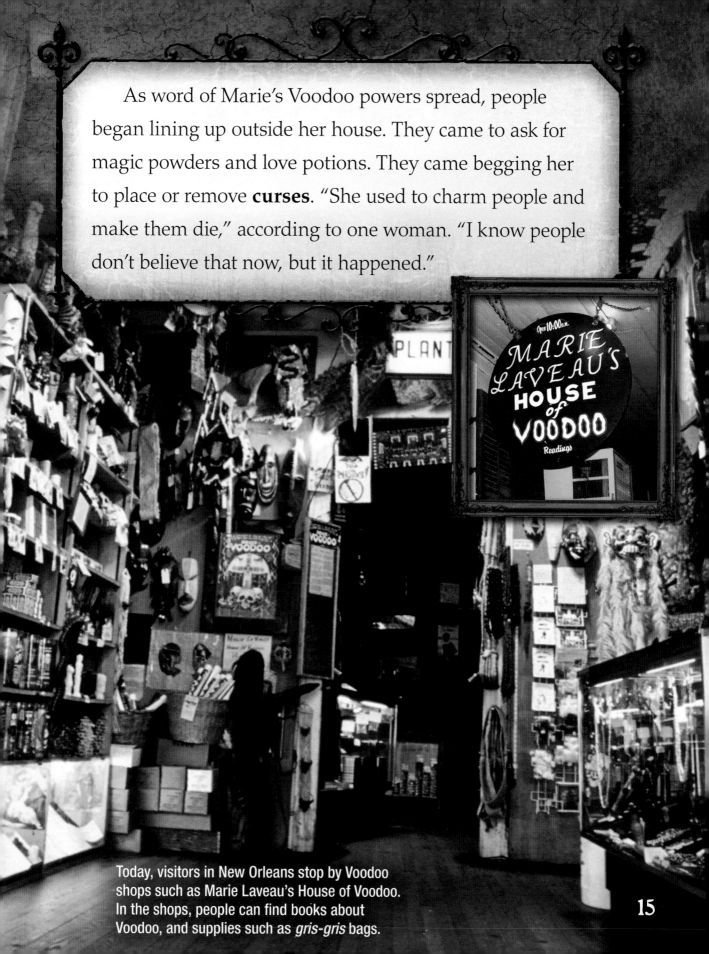

As word of Marie's Voodoo powers spread, people began lining up outside her house. They came to ask for magic powders and love potions. They came begging her to place or remove **curses**. "She used to charm people and make them die," according to one woman. "I know people don't believe that now, but it happened."

Today, visitors in New Orleans stop by Voodoo shops such as Marie Laveau's House of Voodoo. In the shops, people can find books about Voodoo, and supplies such as *gris-gris* bags.

The Voodoo Queen

Marie Laveau was the most famous Voodoo Queen in the history of New Orleans. She used her powers to help others—and herself as well. According to one story, a wealthy man's son was about to be tried for murder. The man went to Marie and promised to buy her a house. All she had to do was make sure his son was found innocent.

Marie nursed the sick during outbreaks of **yellow fever** and cholera in New Orleans. She also took care of wounded soldiers during the **Civil War** (1861-1865).

Marie spent the morning of the trial in prayer, with three fire-hot guinea (GIH-nee) peppers in her mouth. Then she walked into the courtroom and dropped the peppers under the judge's chair. Later that day, the judge declared the young man innocent. Soon Marie moved into a fine house on St. Anne Street.

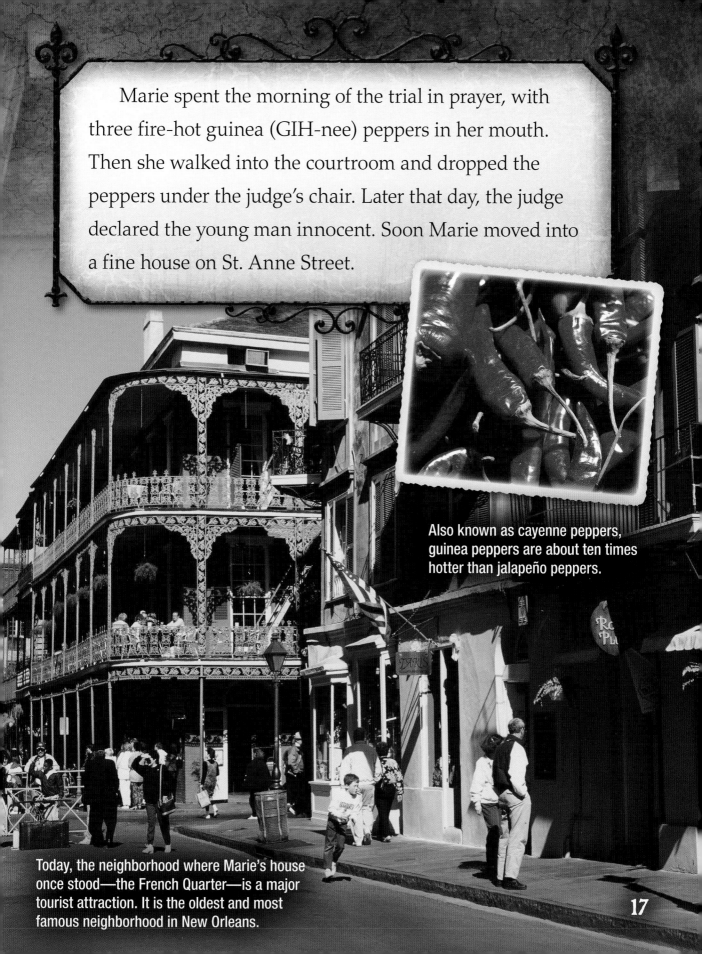

Also known as cayenne peppers, guinea peppers are about ten times hotter than jalapeño peppers.

Today, the neighborhood where Marie's house once stood—the French Quarter—is a major tourist attraction. It is the oldest and most famous neighborhood in New Orleans.

Dancing in Congo Square

For anyone who wanted to see the Voodoo Queen at work, the place to be was Congo Square. Marie held her famous Voodoo ceremonies in this park every Sunday. The police tried to stop her but never succeeded. "She just **hypnotized** them," one witness claimed.

Congo Square, shown here, is now part of Louis Armstrong Park, named for the famous jazz musician who grew up in New Orleans.

After walking into Congo Square, Marie began her Voodoo ceremonies by removing her shoes. Then she lifted a huge, live snake from a box. As the snake wrapped itself around her body, Marie began to dance. Other dancers soon joined in. Around the dancers, people pounded drums and shook tambourines. "Come, great serpent spirit," shouted Marie. "Join us, *le Grand Zombi!*"

Historians believe Marie used a snake called a Louisiana *coluber* in her ceremonies. It may have been about 12 feet (3.6 m) long but was not poisonous.

Marie's snake was called *"le Grand Zombi"*—which is French for "the big Zombie." Snakes were very important to Voodoo as they were believed to represent the great Voodoo spirits.

How to Use Voodoo Dolls

In Voodoo, a powerful way to call upon spirits is by using Voodoo dolls. Voodoo dolls are a form of *gris-gris*. In Hollywood movies, people stick pins in Voodoo dolls to cause pain to their enemies. This is not how dolls were used by traditional Voodoo priestesses such as Marie Laveau, however.

While Marie Laveau made her own dolls, people can buy them ready-made today. Different dolls are designed to help people find love, money, or health.

Voodoo dolls were created to represent a person. Pins were used to attach objects belonging to the person, such as pictures of the person or locks of his or her hair. Someone skilled in Voodoo could then ask spirits to help the person—to bring luck or heal disease, for example.

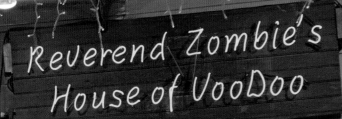

Voodoo shops such as this one in New Orleans sell Voodoo dolls.

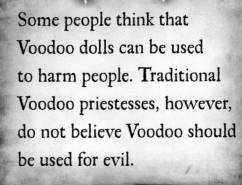

Some people think that Voodoo dolls can be used to harm people. Traditional Voodoo priestesses, however, do not believe Voodoo should be used for evil.

21

Ghosts in the Cathedral

When not dancing with snakes or making Voodoo dolls, Marie Laveau was often seen praying in St. Louis **Cathedral**. Marie mixed her Voodoo with Catholicism, and considered herself a faithful Catholic. She was close friends with **Père** Antoine, the priest of St. Louis Cathedral. This cathedral is the oldest one in the United States. Some say it's also the most haunted.

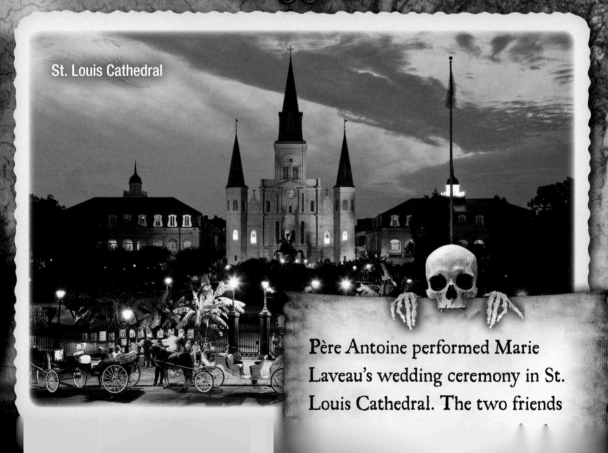

St. Louis Cathedral

Père Antoine performed Marie Laveau's wedding ceremony in St. Louis Cathedral. The two friends

Ever since Antoine's death in 1829, people have reported seeing his ghost. On misty early mornings, he is spotted walking outside the cathedral. It is said that he especially enjoys **choir** practice. He sits in an empty **pew**, a smile on his face, rocking gently to the music.

People who claim to have spotted Père Antoine's ghost report a feeling of warmth and peace, rather than fear.

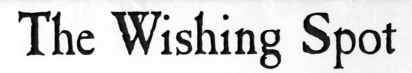

The Wishing Spot

In 1827, Marie Laveau gave birth to a daughter who was also named Marie. Many legends have grown up around this woman. Some people believe that Marie Laveau II learned Voodoo from her mother and became a powerful priestess of Voodoo. Around 1870, so the stories say, Marie Laveau II took over as the new Voodoo Queen of New Orleans.

On Friday afternoons, some people claim that Marie Laveau II held special ceremonies on the banks of Bayou St. John. This place was known as the "Wishing Spot." Here, Marie would pray to the spirits and ask them to help make people's wishes come true. "My grandmother was always talking about it," remembered one woman. "She'd go off on mysterious journeys for a whole day and come back to tell us she had made a wish. The strange part is she always got them."

According to legend, Marie Laveau II led Voodoo celebrations on the banks of Bayou St. John on St. John's Eve, June 23. It is said that she still haunts this area, even today.

The Queen Lives On

The first Marie Laveau died in 1881, at the age of 80. Her body was placed in a tomb in St. Louis Cemetery #1. People have reported seeing her ghost ever since.

Marie's tomb is a popular tourist site in New Orleans. Many people leave gifts for Marie, hoping for help with their problems. Some believe that if they mark three Xs on the tomb with chalk and then knock three times, their wish will be granted.

Some people believe that after dark a giant snake slides out from under Marie Laveau's tomb. They say that the snake wraps itself around the tomb to protect Marie through the night.

In the early 1900s, a man said he was in a store near the cemetery when he noticed an old woman standing beside him. The store owner took one look at the woman, turned, and ran.

The woman threw back her head and let out an enormous laugh. Then she floated into the air and out the door. Terrified, the customer fainted. When he woke up, the store owner was bending over him. "You know who that was?" gasped the astonished owner. "That was Marie Laveau!"

Voodoo ceremonies live on in New Orleans today. They are led by Voodoo priestesses such as Ava Kay Jones.

NEW ORLEANS:
Then and Now

Then: With a population of about 17,000 in 1810, New Orleans was the second-largest city in the South and the sixth-largest in the United States.

Now: Today, Houston, Texas, is the largest city in the South, with about 2 million people. New Orleans ranks 59th in population in the United States, with about 300,000 people.

Then: The first enslaved Africans were brought to New Orleans in the early 1700s. Slavery was legal through most of Marie Laveau's lifetime.

Now: Slavery has been illegal since the adoption of the 13th Amendment to the Constitution in 1865. Today, all people in the United States are free.

New Orleans is sometimes called the Crescent City because part of the city lies along a crescent—or curve—on the Mississippi River.

Then: Marie Laveau and other Voodoo priestesses made Voodoo an important religion in New Orleans.

Now: Voodoo is still practiced in New Orleans. It has also become a tourist attraction, with a Voodoo museum and many shops selling Voodoo supplies.

Then: New Orleans was a deadly city, plagued by natural disasters and killer diseases.

Now: Outbreaks of yellow fever and cholera no longer occur, but hurricanes are still a major threat. In 2005, Hurricane Katrina flooded parts of the city under 15 feet (4.6 m) of water, killing about 1,000 people in Louisiana.

Nearly 500,000 people lived in New Orleans before Hurricane Katrina hit in 2005. The city's population is much lower today, but it is growing quickly once more.

Glossary

balls (BAWLZ) large, fancy parties with dancing

caskets (KASS-kits) containers in which dead bodies are placed for burial

cathedral (kuh-THEE-druhl) a large, important church

cemeteries (SEM-uh-*ter*-eez) areas of land where dead bodies are buried

choir (KWIRE) a singing group; often sings religious music

cholera (KAH-lur-uh) a deadly disease spread through dirty water or food

Civil War (SIV-il WOR) the U.S. war between the Southern states and the Northern states that lasted from 1861 to 1865

communication (kuh-*myoo*-nuh-KAY-shuhn) the sharing of information, wants, needs, and feelings

curses (KURS-iz) things that bring or cause evil or misfortune; spells

hypnotized (HIP-nuh-*tized*) controlled another person's mind by putting them into a trance

Louisiana Purchase (loo-*ee*-zee-AN-uh PUR-chuhss) a land deal made between the United States and France in 1803 in which the United States bought nearly all the land between the Mississippi River and the Rocky Mountains

Native Americans (NAY-tiv uh-MER-uh-kinz) the first people to live in America; they are sometimes called American Indians

peddlers (PED-lurz) people who sell goods in the streets

Père (PAIR) the French word for *father*; used before the name of a priest

pew (PYOO) a church bench

priestess (PREE-stuhss) a female priest

sea level (SEE LEV-uhl) the average height of the sea's surface

settlers (SET-lurz) people who make their home in a new place

sewers (SOO-urz) pipes that carry human waste and dirty water

tombs (TOOMZ) graves, rooms, or buildings in which a dead body is placed

Voodoo (VOO-doo) a religion combining traditional African beliefs with Catholicism

yellow fever (YEL-oh FEE-vur) a deadly disease caused by a virus that is spread through the bite of a mosquito

Bibliography

Sublette, Ned. *The World That Made New Orleans: From Spanish Silver to Congo Square.* Chicago: Lawrence Hill Books (2008).

Tallant, Robert. *Voodoo in New Orleans.* Gretna, LA: Pelican Publishing (2005).

Taylor, Troy. *Haunted New Orleans: Ghosts & Hauntings of the Crescent City.* Alton, IL: Whitechapel Productions Press (2000).

Ward, Martha. *Voodoo Queen: The Spirited Lives of Marie Laveau.* Jackson, MS: University Press of Mississippi (2004).

Read More

Hintz, Martin. *Destination New Orleans.* Minneapolis, MN: Lerner (1997).

Prentzas, G. S. *New Orleans (Cities of the World).* New York: Children's Press (1998).

Strom, Laura Layton. *Built Below Sea Level: New Orleans.* New York: Children's Press (2008).

Learn More Online

To learn more about New Orleans and Voodoo, visit
www.bearportpublishing.com/HorrorScapes

Index

About the Author

Stephen Person has written many children's books about history, science, and the environment. He lives with his family in Brooklyn, New York.